D1519539

SandCastle™

Baby
African Animals

It's a Baby Lion!

Kelly Doudna

Consulting Editor, Diane Craig, M.A./Reading Specialist

ABDO
Publishing Company

Published by ABDO Publishing Company, 8000 West 78th Street, Edina, Minnesota 55439.

Printed in the United States.

Editor: Liz Salzmann
Content Developer: Nancy Tuminelly
Cover and Interior Design and Production: Mighty Media
Photo Credits: Comstock, Digital Vision, iStockPhoto (David Gomez), Peter Arnold Inc. (Michel & Christine Denis-Huot, TUNS), ShutterStock

Library of Congress Cataloging-in-Publication Data

Doudna, Kelly, 1963-
 It's a baby lion! / Kelly Doudna.
    p. cm. -- (Baby African animals)
 ISBN 978-1-60453-156-5
 1. Lions--Infancy--Juvenile literature. I. Title.

QL737.C23D585 2009
599.757'139--dc22
                        2008007015

SandCastle™ Level: Transitional

SandCastle™ books are created by a team of professional educators, reading specialists, and content developers around five essential components—phonemic awareness, phonics, vocabulary, text comprehension, and fluency—to assist young readers as they develop reading skills and strategies and increase their general knowledge. All books are written, reviewed, and leveled for guided reading, early reading intervention, and Accelerated Reader® programs for use in shared, guided, and independent reading and writing activities to support a balanced approach to literacy instruction. The SandCastle™ series has four levels that correspond to early literacy development. The levels are provided to help teachers and parents select appropriate books for young readers.

Emerging Readers	**Beginning Readers**	**Transitional Readers**	**Fluent Readers**
(no flags)	(1 flag)	(2 flags)	(3 flags)

SandCastle™ would like to hear from you. Please send us your comments and suggestions.
sandcastle@abdopublishing.com

Vital Statistics

for the Lion

BABY NAME
cub

NUMBER IN LITTER
1 to 6, average 3 to 4

WEIGHT AT BIRTH
3 pounds

AGE OF INDEPENDENCE
1½ to 2 years

ADULT WEIGHT
265 to 550 pounds

LIFE EXPECTANCY
14 years

Lions are the only cats that live in groups. A group of lions is called a pride.

Lion cubs are born blind and helpless. Their eyes open when they are 11 days old.

Cubs are born with spots that fade as they get older.

A female lion is a lioness.
Every lioness helps raise
all of the cubs in the pride.

Cubs nurse from any
lioness, not just their
mothers.

Male lions from outside the pride are the main enemy of lion cubs.

The fathers protect the cubs from male lions that are not from their pride.

Cubs begin to roar when they are one year old.

A lion's roar can be heard five miles away. It's a way they mark their territory.

Lions rub heads to bond with each other.

Lionesses stay with their birth pride for life. Male lions leave when they are two or three.

Fun Fact

About the Lion

Adult lions can eat up to 15 pounds of meat per day. That's like 60 quarter-pound hamburgers!

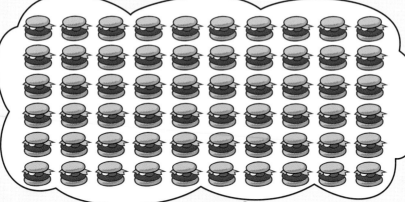

Glossary

birth – 1) the moment when a person or animal is born. 2) having to do with being born.

bond – to form a connection with another.

carnivore – one who eats meat.

expectancy – an expected or likely amount.

fade – to slowly disappear.

independence – no longer needing others to care for or support you.

nurse – to feed a baby milk from the breast.

pride – a group of lions that live, travel, and feed together.

protect – to guard someone or something from harm or danger.

quarter-pound – weighing one-fourth of one pound.

territory – an area that is occupied and defended by an animal or a group of animals.

To see a complete list of SandCastle™ books and other nonfiction titles from ABDO Publishing Company, visit **www.abdopublishing.com**.

8000 West 78th Street, Edina, MN 55439

800-800-1312 • 952-831-1632 fax